Will Shortz Presents

I CAN KENKEN!

Volume 1

KenKen™: Logic Puzzles That Make You Smarter!

Will Shortz Presents KenKen Easiest, Volume 1
Will Shortz Presents KenKen Easy, Volume 2
Will Shortz Presents KenKen Easy to Hard, Volume 3
Will Shortz Presents The Little Gift Book of KenKen

KenKen for Kids

Will Shortz Presents I Can KenKen! Volume 1
Will Shortz Presents I Can KenKen! Volume 2
Will Shortz Presents I Can KenKen! Volume 3

Will Shortz Presents

I Can KENKEN!™

VOLUME 1

75 PUZZLES FOR HAVING FUN WITH MATH

TETSUYA MIYAMOTO

Introduction by
MARILYN BURNS

ST. MARTIN'S GRIFFIN
NEW YORK

WILL SHORTZ PRESENTS I CAN KENKEN! VOLUME I. Copyright © 2008 by Gakken Co., Ltd. All rights reserved. Printed in the United States of America. For information, address St. Martin's Press, 175 Fifth Avenue, New York, N.Y. 10010.

www.stmartins.com

ISBN-13: 978-0-312-54641-0
ISBN-10: 0-312-54641-6

D 20 19 18 17 16 15 14 13 12 11

Foreword

Lots of things in life that are good for you aren't much fun. For example, taking a bath, doing homework, getting a flu shot, going to the dentist, or eating [name any nutritious food you hate].

Conversely, lots of things in life that are fun aren't good for you, like . . . well, you can make your own list!

Then there are a few things you absolutely love—no one has to tell you to do them—that improve your health, your mind, your schoolwork, or your future.

One such thing is KenKen, a new puzzle from Japan that involves logic and numbers. I fell in love with it when I first saw it a year ago. Now, here is a whole book of KenKen puzzles to do!

The rules are simple (keep reading). You can start solving in thirty seconds, but KenKen takes a long time to master.

If you're like me, you won't want to put it down. At the same time as you're enjoying yourself, KenKen will sharpen your mind and improve your arithmetic skills.

If only every good thing in the world were this much fun!

—Will Shortz

Introduction

If you like solving puzzles, then this book is definitely for you.

But . . . if you think that solving puzzles isn't your kind of thing to do, don't give up on this book too quickly. KenKen puzzles may help you change your mind.

Read on.

Why Solve KenKen Puzzles?

Here are reasons from kids who have learned how to KenKen. See if any of these tempt you to give KenKen puzzles a try.

"They're super fun."

"It feels really, really good when you finish one."

"I like KenKen puzzles because they wake up your brain."

"You can tell by yourself if you get the puzzle right."

"There are different ways to figure them out."

"It's fun to look for clues."

"I think KenKen is really cool."

Maybe you can add your own reason after you try KenKen puzzles for yourself.

In the meantime, here's some help to get you started.

What Are KenKen Puzzles?

KenKen puzzles are puzzles you solve by writing a number in each box on a grid. The numbers you are allowed to write depend on the size of the grid. If the puzzle is a 3×3 grid with three boxes across and three boxes down, you can only fill in the numbers 1, 2, and 3. If the puzzle is a 4×4 grid, you can only fill in the numbers 1, 2, 3, and 4. For a 5×5 puzzle, you can only fill in the numbers 1, 2, 3, 4, and, 5. And for a 6×6 puzzle, you can fill in the numbers 1, 2, 3, 4, 5, 6. That's the easy part.

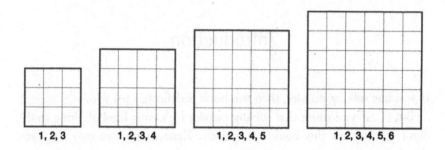

| 1, 2, 3 | 1, 2, 3, 4 | 1, 2, 3, 4, 5 | 1, 2, 3, 4, 5, 6 |

The harder part is figuring out *where* to write the numbers. There is one **Basic Rule** you must follow to solve the puzzle:

When you fill in the numbers in a KenKen puzzle, each row going across has to have exactly one of each of the numbers. No repeats are allowed. And the same is true for the columns—each column going down has to have exactly one of the numbers you can write, with no repeats.

The good news is that you don't have to worry about the numbers on the diagonals, just about the numbers in the rows and columns.

OK

1	2	3
3	1	2
2	3	1

Not OK

1	2	3
2	1	3
3	2	1

But there's another challenge to solving KenKen puzzles. Not only do you have to follow the Basic Rule, you also have to follow the special Number Clues. All of the puzzles in this book are Addition KenKen puzzles. Let's look at the following puzzle. It's a 3×3 Addition KenKen puzzle.

See the different shapes on the puzzle grid outlined with dark lines? And see that each outlined shape has a number written in the upper left corner? These are the special **Number Clues.**

First, the Number Clues that are in outlined one-box shapes: These are lucky clues! Each of these boxes is a freebie. The Number Clue gives you the number to write in that box. That's it. Even though this is Addition KenKen, no adding is needed. (That's why these are freebies!) Find the two freebies in this puzzle. (Both freebies in this puzzle are number 1, but the freebies can be any of the numbers you're allowed to write.)

Now about the other Number Clues: When a number is in an outlined shape with more than one box, the number is a sum, or total, you get when you add. (Remember, this is an Addition KenKen puzzle.) Here's what these Number Clues tell you:

1. First look at the Number Clue 3 in the upper left corner of the puzzle. See how this clue is in the outlined two-box shape? This Number Clue tells you that the two numbers you write in this shape,

one in each box, have to *add up* to 3. (Remember, Number Clues are sums, or totals. Don't be confused to think that you are supposed to add 3 to a number—you have to think of two numbers that *add up* to 3.)

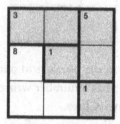

2. Now look at the puzzle again and find the Number Clue 8. This clue is in the outlined three-box shape that sort of looks like the letter L. It tells you that the three numbers you write in this shape, one in each box, have to add up to 8.

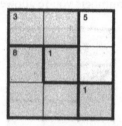

3. And when the Number Clue is 5—as in the box in the upper right corner of the puzzle—then the two numbers you write in this shape, one in each box, have to add up to 5.

Remember:
   1. Follow the **Basic Rule** and be sure to write numbers without repeats in any row or column.
   2. Follow the special **Number Clues** in the outlined shapes.

How to Get Started Solving a KenKen Puzzle
Now let's solve this puzzle. Here are suggestions for getting started.

Check for freebies. This is a good first step. When you're lucky to have a freebie—one box outlined with a number in it—take advantage of the hint and write that number in the box. You don't have to do any math. Be sure to check to see if a puzzle has more than one freebie. This puzzle has two freebies, both 1s, so you can write these numbers in the puzzle.

Use the Number Clues. Let's start at the top with the Number Clue 3 in a two-box shape. Remember, since this is a 3×3 puzzle, the only numbers you are allowed to write in the boxes are 1, 2, and 3. Only two of those numbers add up to 3: 1+2. But . . . before you write the numbers 1 and 2 in the boxes, you have to figure out which number goes in which box. You want to be sure to follow the Basic Rule.

Look for other clues. Other numbers already in the puzzle, like the freebies, can give useful clues. Here the freebie in the middle box is a *big* help. Because the middle box has a 1 in it, you can't write a 1 in the box above it. That would put two 1s in the same column and break the Basic

Rule. That's a definite no-no. So, when you write the numbers 1 and 2 in the shape with the Number Clue 3, you have to write the 1 in the first box and the 2 in the second box. Can you explain why this is right?

³1	2	⁵3
⁸	¹1	
	3	¹1

Keep an eye out for "automatic" numbers. Sometimes you have written all but one number in a row or column. Then you can use the Basic Rule to see which number is missing, without having to do any other figuring. In this puzzle, the top row across already has a 1 and a 2 in it, so the last box has to be a 3. It's automatic. And the middle column going down already has a 2 and a 1 in it, so the bottom box has to be a 3. Can you explain why this is right?

³1	2	⁵3
⁸	¹1	2
	3	¹1

To finish this puzzle, you have to look for more clues. Look at the two-box shape on the right. There's already a 3 in it, and the Number Clue is 5, so the number in the other box has to be a 2. Or you could reason that the 2 is automatic. Can you explain why this is right?

³1	2	⁵3
⁸3	¹1	2
2	3	¹1

And you can use the automatic strategy to fill in the missing numbers.

Some Helpful Tips

Here are some things to think about when you're solving KenKen puzzles.

- Don't rush! Solving a KenKen puzzle is not a race. The idea is to be right, not fast. Take your time, and check as you go.
- When you write an "automatic" number, be sure to check that you've also followed the clues and the numbers you wrote add up to the Number Clue in the shape. In the puzzle we just solved, this means being sure that the three numbers in the L-shape at the bottom left corner, $3+2+3$, add up to 8. (They do!)
- Use pencil. We all make mistakes, and being able to erase is really handy. (Don't worry about making mistakes—mistakes can always help you learn more about a puzzle.) After you've solved a KenKen puzzle, you can trace over the numbers with a pen, marker, or crayon.
- It often helps to figure out all the possible combinations of numbers that might work for the boxes in a shape. Say you are solving a 4×4 KenKen puzzle. For this puzzle you can write the numbers 1, 2, 3, and 4. In the puzzle on the next page, see the Number Clue 5 in the two-box shape in the top row?

It tells you that the two numbers in this shape have to add up to 5. If you think about both the numbers and the order you write them, there are four choices:

$2+3$

$3+2$

$1+4$

$4+1$

The challenge is to look for other clues to help you figure out the numbers and where to write them.

Try solving this 4×4 puzzle now. Use the **How to Get Started** suggestions. Remember that the first suggestion is to write in the freebies. After you do this, use them as clues to decide about the shape in the top row with the Number Clue 5.

When You've Solved a Puzzle

Whenever you write numbers in all of the boxes in a KenKen puzzle, be sure to do a check. First be sure that you've followed the Basic Rule and there are no repeat numbers in any row or column.

Then be sure that your numbers follow the Number Clues and your math is correct.

For a final check, you can add the numbers in each row and column. You should get the same sum each time. In a 3×3 KenKen puzzle, the numbers in each row and column add up to 6; in a 4×4 puzzle, they add up to 10; in a 5×5 puzzle, they add up to 15; in a 6×6 puzzle, they add up to 21.

And to be absolutely sure, you can check the puzzle answer at the back of the book.

The KenKen Code

For many, many years, mathematicians have written QED at the end of the solution to a problem. This was a signal to show that they worked on the problem, got it done, and checked to be sure the solution was right. Why QED? The letters stand for the words in a sentence written in Latin—*quod erat demonstratum*. In English, this means that you have proved something to be true.

When you solve a KenKen puzzle and have checked that you are right, you can write our special KenKen signal—ICKK. Or just say the letters—I-C-K-K. This is KenKen code for QED. In English, it means "I can KenKen!"

¹1	⁷4	⁵3	2
⁷4	3	²2	⁵1
3	²2	⁵1	4
³2	1	4	³3

Check the Stars on the KenKen Puzzles

You'll see that each KenKen puzzle in this book is marked with one star, two stars, or three stars. That's to tell you whether the puzzle is **easy** (one star), **medium** (two stars), or **hard** (three stars). All of the 3×3 KenKen puzzles are one-star puzzles. But the size of the puzzle isn't the only thing that matters. For example, easier puzzles usually have more freebies. And harder puzzles usually have more possibilities for the numbers that can work in the boxes. So some 4×4 KenKen puzzles are easy, some are medium, and some are hard. And the same is true for 5×5 KenKen puzzles and 6×6 KenKen puzzles.

Pick puzzles to solve in any way you'd like. You may want to try all of the one-star puzzles first. Or you may want to solve the puzzles by size. Or solve the KenKen puzzles in no order at all.

Now you're ready to KenKen! Have fun!

P.S. If you'd like to try KenKen puzzles where you have to multiply, or KenKen puzzles where you have to both add and subtract, check out volumes 2 and 3 of the I Can KenKen! books.

Difficulty Level

 Easy

 Medium

 Hard

5
3

3
1

2

3
2

3
3

4
1

3
1

2

3

Let the KenKen begin!

2 +

3 2	**4** 1	3
1	**5** 3	**3** 2
3 3	2	2

+ **3**

1 1	**8** 3	2
5 2	**1** 1	3
3	**3** 2	1

3	3	
3	1	2
6		
1	2	3
5		1
2	3	1

+ **5**

3 2	**5** 3	**1** 1
1	2	**5** 3
4 3	1	2

4	8	
3	3	2
2	1	3
6		
3	2	1

+ **7**

5		1	11
3	2	1	4
3	**5**		
2	1	4	3
		5	
1	4	3	2
7		**3**	
4	3	2	1

5		3	3
2	4	3	1
4	**5**	**3**	
4	3	1	2
5			**4**
3	2	2	4
	1	**7**	
2	1	4	3

+ **9**

1 1	**7** 4	3	**3** 2
7 4	**3** 3	**3** 2	1
3	**3** 2	1	**7** 4
2 2	1	**4** 4	3

3 3	**3** 2	1	**7** 4
3 2	**1** 1	**7** 4	3
1	**7** 4	3	**2** 2
4 4	3	**3** 2	1

7 3	2 2	3 1	4 4
4	7 3	2	3 1
3 1	4	3 3	2
2	5 4	1	3 3

12 + ★

3	5	3	
3	**5** 4	**3** 1	2
5 4	1	**2** 2	**7** 3
1	**2** 2	**7** 3	4
5 2	3	4	**1** 1

+ **13**

5	5		4
1	3	2	4
3		**4**	
4	2	2	3
5		**4**	**3**
3	1	4	2
	7		
2	4	3	1

14 +

5 1	5 2	3	4 4
4	5 1	5 2	3
3 3	4	5 1	3 2
5 2	3	4	1

+ **15**

5 1	5 3	6 4	2
4	2	5 3	1 1
5 3	1 1	2	7 4
2	5 4	1	3

16 +

4 1	**2** 2	**7** 3	**4**
3	**5** 4	**3** 1	**5** 2
6 4	1	2	3
2	**7** 3	4	**1** 1

6 3	2	1	**9** 4
3 2	**1** 1	**7** 4	3
1	**7** 4	3	2
4 4	3	**3** 2	1

Remember, fill in "freebies" first!

18 +

3 1	**7** 4	3	**5** 2
2	**3** 1	**4** 4	3
7 3	2	**5** 1	4
4	**3** 3	**3** 2	1

+ **19**

3 3	**7** 4 4	**8** 1 1	**3** 2
3 2	3 3	4 1	1
1	**2** 2	8	**7** 4
7 4	~~1~~	2	3

3 3	**7** 4	**7** 2	1
7 2	3	**1** 1	4
8	**6** 2	4	**5** 3
4	**4** 1	3	4

9 3	4	**3** 1	2
2	**3** 3	**5** 4	1
6 1	**5** 2	3	**4** 4
4	1	**5** 2 3	3

22 +

7		3	7
	1	2	*3*	
				4

7	5	3	
	4	4	2	3

3			7
3			
		4	1	2

| 5 | | | |
| | 2 | 3 | 4 | 1 |

+ **23**

4	**7**		**6**
1	4	3	2
3			
3	2	3	4
6	**4**	**3**	
4	3	2	1
		7	
2	1	4	3

24 + ⭐ ⭐

4		6	
7	3	4	
		3	7
6			

+ **25**

6	7		6
	4		
		4	6
7			

6		7	3
3	7		
		4	
4		6	

+ **27**

8	9		
	3	4	
		3	7
6			

28 +

9	6		
	3	5	
		9	
8			

+ **29**

7			5
5		6	
7	5		
		5	

30 +

3	7	4	
		7	3
6			
4		6	

+ **31**

7	8		
	5		9
	8	3	

32 +

5		5	
8	3		7
	5		
	7		

3		12	
8	9		
			5
	3		

8			5
5	5		
		12	
5			

★ ★ ★   + **35**

7	6		
	4		9
3		11	

36 +

17+	3+		7+	
		3+		3
	8+	4	6+	
		9+		7+
	4	4+		

+ **37**

12+	10+	8+		4+
		6+	1	
			11+	9+
3+		1		
	8+			2

38 +

9+			2	6+
9+	3+	8+		
			8+	4+
5+	9+			
	4	8+		

+ **39**

5+		7+		7+
11+		3+		
	2	9+		3+
9+		4+		
3+		4	8+	

40 +

7+		3+		7+
9+	3+	7+		
		5	8+	5+
3+	5+			
	9+		4+	

+ **41**

6+			13+	
5	6+		6+	
12+				
5+		13+		6+
3+				

42 +

12+	3+		10+	
	10+	3+		
		9+	6+	
7+			6+	
		4+		5

+ **43**

9+	7+		5+	
	6+			8+
10+				
3+	7+		9+	6+
	5			

44 +

9+	3+		8+	
	14+	3+		3
		9+		3+
3+		7+		
	8+		5+	

+ 45

6+	10+		7+	
	8+		9+	4+
		6+		
7+			3+	
4+		4	7+	

46 +

9+	10+	3	15+	
		6+		
			11+	3
11+				7+

+ **47**

9+		5+	14+	4
7+				6+
		7+		
9+				5+
	9+			

48 +

14+	3+	16+		
		8+		
	13+	2		9+
10+				

+ **49**

8+	8+		13+	
	3+			
	12+	9+	3	3+
			11+	
	5+			

50 +

9+		10+		
7+		11+	8+	
3+				
		9+		9+
7+		2		

+ **51**

8+		6+	6+	
9+			6+	7+
	3+			
10+			7+	
	9+		4+	

52 +

3+	6+		8+	
	10+	6+		9+
5		7+		
7+		3+		
	5+		6+	

+ **53**

6+		6+		13+
10+				
3+	7+	7+		
		10+	3	
8+				2

+

3+	14+		6+	
			8+	
8+	6+		9+	
	5+			7+
9+				

+ 55

3+		**9+**		**4+**
9+		**5+**		
5+		**5+**	**6+**	
8+			**13+**	
	8+			

56 +

8+	5+	5	12+		
		12+	9+		3+
10+			3+	16+	
3+					
	11+		8+	5+	7+
6	3+				

Level up! Now you use numbers 1, 2, 3, 4, 5, and 6!

+ **57**

3+	7+		11+		6+
	11+	12+	7+		
11+			3+	5+	
	6+			7+	
7+			7+		8+
	6+		9+		

58 +

3	11+		7+		
3+		8+	11+		8+
11+			7+	3+	
	11+				5+
10+			8+		
	6+		8+		6

+ **59**

11+		**6**	**4+**		**7+**
	9+	**3+**		**8+**	
9+		**11+**			**3+**
	4+	**9+**		**8+**	
3+		**5+**			**15+**
	11+				

6+	3+		10+	10+	
	11+				6+
11+		4+		8+	
5+		11+			4+
7+	1		11+		
	10+		2	6+	

+ 61

3+	**10+**	**5+**	**6+**		**11+**
			7+	**4+**	
11+		**4**			**5+**
8+		**11+**	**6**		
8+			**7+**	**10+**	**7+**
	3+				

62 +

7+	13+				5+
	6+		11+		
14+	3+		9+		8+
		11+	6+		
8+				12+	
	10+		3+		

+ 63

6+	11+	12+		5+	
		7+			9+
8+	7+		3+		
		10+	11+		3+
7+	3+		16+		
				8+	

64 +

3+	11+	8+		8+	
11+	7+	13+			5+
11+	7+			11+	
	3+		4		
10+		9+		5	13+
	5+				

+ **65**

6	7+		8+		
3+		13+	10+		7+
8+	11+		6+		
				3+	10+
9+		8+			
	3+		14+		

66 +

5+ 3	2	6+		14+	
6+		7+	11+		3+
9+				7+	
10+		7+	5+		11+
	1			7+	
11+		6+			

+ **67**

14+		5+		7+	
6+		4+	12+		
	3+		11+	3	7+
9+		11+		9+	
	4		7+		
	8+			6+	

8+		15+			
4	6+	15+			
11+	4+		18+		6+
				7+	
9+					8+
15+					

+ **69**

3+	11+	8+		10+	
		8+	6+		7+
10+					
8+	3+		10+		11+
	8+	13+		8+	
			2		

70 +

15+			7+		10+
9+		10+		7+	
		3+	7+		
11+				3+	11+
4	11+	11+			
			7+		

+ **71**

13+	6+	5+		11+	
		8+	10+		15+
9+		3+		10+	
15+					
5+		13+			3

72 +

12+	3+		10+	12+	
	11+				
	8+		3+	8+	10+
7+		6+			
10+			11+		
		11+		4+	

★ ★ ★   **+ 73**

8+	8+		7+		1
		15+			5+
15+			4+		
7+		12+		8+	9+
6+					
3	5+		13+		

74 +

7+	3	9+	12+		
			9+		3+
11+	7+		8+	9+	
	3+				7+
9+		14+	3+		
			12+		

+ 75

14+			6+		6+
15+	3	10+			
	3+	7+		7+	
		7+			15+
6+		11+			
10+				6	

CONGRATULATIONS!

_____

(print name here)

You have just completed
I Can KenKen! Volume 1!
In doing so, you mastered seventy-five
killer KenKen puzzles from small 3×3 grids to
giant 6×6 grids using addition.

YOU'VE OFFICIALLY ACHIEVED THE RANK OF

KENKEN CAPTAIN

ANSWERS

1

⁵3	³1	2
2	³3	⁴1
³1	2	3

2

³2	⁴1	3
1	⁵3	³2
³3	2	1

3

¹1	⁸3	2
⁵2	¹1	3
3	³2	1

4

³3	³1	2
⁶1	2	3
⁵2	3	¹1

5

³2	⁵3	¹1
1	2	⁵3
⁴3	1	2

6

⁴1	⁸3	2
2	1	3
⁶3	2	1

7

⁵3	2	¹1	¹¹4
³2	⁵1	4	3
1	4	⁵3	2
⁷4	3	³2	1

8

⁵1	4	³3	³2
⁴4	⁵3	³2	1
⁵3	2	1	⁴4
2	¹1	⁷4	3

9

¹1	⁷4	3	³2
⁷4	³3	³2	1
3	³2	1	⁷4
²2	1	⁴4	3

10

³3	³2	1	⁷4
³2	¹1	⁷4	3
1	⁷4	3	²2
⁴4	3	³2	1

11

⁷3	²2	³1	⁴4
4	⁷3	2	³1
³1	4	³3	2
2	⁵1	4	³3

12

³3	⁵4	³1	2
⁵4	1	²2	⁷3
1	²2	⁷3	4
⁵2	3	4	¹1

13

⁵1	⁵3	2	⁴4
4	³2	⁴1	3
⁵3	1	⁴4	³2
2	⁷4	3	1

14

⁵1	⁵2	3	⁴4
4	⁵1	⁵2	3
³3	4	⁵1	³2
⁵2	3	4	1

15

⁵1	⁵3	⁶4	2
4	2	⁵3	¹1
⁵3	¹1	2	⁷4
2	⁵4	1	3

16

⁴1	²2	⁷3	4
3	⁵4	³1	⁵2
⁶4	1	2	3
2	⁷3	4	¹1

17

⁶3	2	1	⁹4
³2	¹1	⁷4	3
1	⁷4	3	2
⁴4	3	³2	1

18

³1	⁷4	3	⁵2
2	³1	⁴4	3
⁷3	2	⁵1	4
4	³3	³2	1

19

3	4	1	2
2	3	4	1
1	2	3	4
4	1	2	3

20

3	4	2	1
2	3	1	4
1	2	4	3
4	1	3	2

21

3	4	1	2
2	3	4	1
1	2	3	4
4	1	2	3

22

1	2	3	4
4	1	2	3
3	4	1	2
2	3	4	1

23

1	4	3	2
3	2	1	4
4	3	2	1
2	1	4	3

24

1	3	4	2
4	2	3	1
3	1	2	4
2	4	1	3

25

6	7		6
2	3	4	1
4	1 [4]	2	3
1	2	3 [4]	4 [6]
3 [7]	4	1	2

26

6		7	3
4	2	3	1
1 [3]	3 [7]	4	2
2	4	1 [4]	3
3 [4]	1	2 [6]	4

27

8	9		
1	3	4	2
4	2 [3]	3 [4]	1
3	1	2 [3]	4 [7]
2 [6]	4	1	3

28

9	6		
4	3	2	1
3	2 [3]	1 [5]	4
2	1	4 [9]	3
1 [8]	4	3	2

29

7			5
2	1	4	3
1 [5]	4	3 [6]	2
4 [7]	3 [5]	2	1
3	2	1 [5]	4

30

3	7	4	
2	4	1	3
1	3	4 [7]	2 [3]
4 [6]	2	3	1
3 [4]	1	2 [6]	4

31

7 2	8 3	4	1
1	5 2	3	9 4
4	8 1	3 2	3
3	4	1	2

32

5 2	3	5 4	1
8 4	3 1	2	7 3
1	5 2	3	4
3	7 4	1	2

33

3 2	1	12 4	3
8 1	9 4	3	2
4	3	2	5 1
3	3 2	1	4

34

8 3	4	1	5 2
5 4	5 1	2	3
1	2	12 3	4
5 2	3	4	1

35

7 4	6 3	2	1
3	4 2	1	9 4
3 2	1	11 4	3
1	4	3	2

36

17+ 5	3+ 1	2	7+ 3	4
4	5	3+ 1	2	3 3
3	8+ 2	4 4	6+ 5	1
1	3	9+ 5	4	7+ 2
2	4 4	4+ 3	1	5

37

12+ 4	10+ 2	8+ 5	3	4+ 1
5	4	6+ 2	1 1	3
3	1	4	11+ 2	9+ 5
3+ 2	3	1 1	5	4
1	8+ 5	3	4	2 2

38

9+ 1	3	5	2 2	6+ 4
9+ 5	3+ 1	8+ 3	4	2
4	2	1	8+ 5	4+ 3
5+ 2	9+ 5	4	3	1
3	4 4	8+ 2	1	5

39

5+ 1	4	7+ 2	5	7+ 3
11+ 5	3	3+ 1	2	4
3	2 2	9+ 5	4	3+ 1
9+ 4	5	4+ 3	1	2
3+ 2	1	4 4	8+ 3	5

40

7+ 3	4	3+ 1	2	7+ 5
9+ 5	3+ 1	7+ 3	4	2
4	2	5 5	8+ 3	5+ 1
3+ 1	5+ 3	2	5	4
2	9+ 5	4	4+ 1	3

41

6+ 2	3	1	13+ 4	5
5 5	6+ 4	2	6+ 1	3
12+ 3	5	4	2	1
5+ 4	1	13+ 5	3	6+ 2
3+ 1	2	3	5	4

42

12+ 5	3+ 1	2	10+ 3	4
4	10+ 5	3+ 1	2	3
3	2	9+ 4	6+ 5	1
7+ 1	3	5	6+ 4	2
2	4	4+ 3	1	5 5

43

4	2	5	3	1
5	4	2	1	3
3	1	4	2	5
2	3	1	5	4
1	5	3	4	2

44

4	1	2	3	5
5	4	1	2	3
3	2	4	5	1
1	5	3	4	2
2	3	5	1	4

45

1	5	2	3	4
5	2	3	4	1
2	4	1	5	3
4	3	5	1	2
3	1	4	2	5

46

1	2	3	5	4
3	4	2	1	5
5	1	4	2	3
2	3	5	4	1
4	5	1	3	2

47

3	2	1	5	4
2	1	4	3	5
5	3	2	4	1
1	4	5	2	3
4	5	3	1	2

48

2	1	4	5	3
5	2	1	3	4
3	5	2	4	1
4	3	5	1	2
1	4	3	2	5

49

8+ 1	8+ 5	3	13+ 2	4
5	3+ 2	1	4	3
2	12+ 4	9+ 5	3 3	3+ 1
3	1	4	11+ 5	2
4	5+ 3	2	1	5

50

9+ 4	5	10+ 1	3	2
7+ 5	2	11+ 3	8+ 1	4
3+ 1	3	4	2	5
2	1	9+ 5	4	9+ 3
7+ 3	4	2 2	5	1

51

8+ 3	5	6+ 1	6+ 4	2
9+ 5	2	3	6+ 1	7+ 4
4	3+ 1	2	5	3
10+ 1	3	4	7+ 2	5
2	9+ 4	5	4+ 3	1

52

3+ 1	6+ 2	4	8+ 3	5
2	10+ 4	6+ 5	1	9+ 3
5 5	1	7+ 3	4	2
7+ 3	5	3+ 1	2	4
4	5+ 3	2	6+ 5	1

53

6+ 5	1	6+ 4	2	13+ 3
10+ 4	2	3	1	5
3+ 1	7+ 3	7+ 2	5	4
2	4	10+ 5	3 3	1
8+ 3	5	1	4	2 2

54

3+ 2	14+ 3	4	6+ 1	5
1	2	5	8+ 3	4
8+ 3	6+ 4	2	9+ 5	1
5	5+ 1	3	4	7+ 2
9+ 4	5	1	2	3

55

3+ 2	1	9+ 5	4	4+ 3
9+ 5	4	5+ 2	3	1
5+ 3	2	5+ 4	6+ 1	5
8+ 4	3	1	13+ 5	2
1	8+ 5	3	2	4

56

8+ 3	5+ 1	5 5	12+ 4	2	6
5	4	12+ 2	9+ 6	3	3+ 1
10+ 4	6	3	3+ 1	16+ 5	2
3+ 1	3	4	2	6	5
2	11+ 5	6	8+ 3	5+ 1	7+ 4
6 6	3+ 2	1	5	4	3

57

3+ 2	7+ 3	4	11+ 6	5	6+ 1
1	11+ 6	12+ 2	7+ 4	3	5
11+ 6	5	3	3+ 2	5+ 1	4
5	6+ 2	6	1	7+ 4	3
7+ 3	4	1	7+ 5	2	8+ 6
4	6+ 1	5	9+ 3	6	2

58

3 3	11+ 6	5	7+ 1	4	2
3+ 2	1	8+ 4	11+ 6	5	8+ 3
11+ 6	3	1	7+ 4	3+ 2	5
5	11+ 2	6	3	1	5+ 4
10+ 4	5	3	8+ 2	6	1
1	6+ 4	2	8+ 5	3	6 6

59

11+ 5	2	6 6	4+ 3	1	7+ 4
4	9+ 5	3+ 2	1	8+ 6	3
9+ 3	4	11+ 5	6	2	3+ 1
6	4+ 1	9+ 4	5	3	2
3+ 2	3	5+ 1	4	5	15+ 6
1	11+ 6	3	2	4	5

60

6+ 5	3+ 2	1	10+ 3	10+ 4	6
1	11+ 6	5	4	3	6+ 2
11+ 6	5	4+ 3	1	8+ 2	4
5+ 2	3	11+ 4	5	6	4+ 1
7+ 4	1 1	2	11+ 6	5	3
3	10+ 4	6	2 2	6+ 1	5

61

2 (3+)	**4** (10+)	**3** (5+)	**1** (6+)	**5**	**6** (11+)
1	**6**	**2**	**4** (7+)	**3** (4+)	**5**
6 (11+)	**5**	**4** (4)	**3**	**1**	**2** (5+)
4 (8+)	**3**	**5** (11+)	**6** (6)	**2**	**1**
5 (8+)	**1**	**6**	**2** (7+)	**4** (10+)	**3** (7+)
3	**2** (3+)	**1**	**5**	**6**	**4**

62

6 (7+)	**1** (13+)	**3**	**5**	**4**	**2** (5+)
1	**4** (6+)	**2**	**6** (11+)	**5**	**3**
5 (14+)	**2** (3+)	**1**	**3** (9+)	**6**	**4** (8+)
4	**5**	**6** (11+)	**2** (6+)	**3**	**1**
2 (8+)	**3**	**5**	**4**	**1** (12+)	**6**
3	**6** (10+)	**4**	**1** (3+)	**2**	**5**

63

5 (6+)	**6** (11+)	**3** (12+)	**2**	**1** (5+)	**4**
1	**5**	**2** (7+)	**3**	**4**	**6** (9+)
6 (8+)	**4** (7+)	**5**	**1** (3+)	**2**	**3**
2	**3**	**4** (10+)	**5** (11+)	**6**	**1** (3+)
3 (7+)	**1** (3+)	**6**	**4** (16+)	**5**	**2**
4	**2**	**1**	**6**	**3** (8+)	**5**

64

1 (3+)	**5** (11+)	**2** (8+)	**6**	**4** (8+)	**3**
2	**6**	**5** (13+)	**3**	**1**	**4** (5+)
6 (11+)	**4** (7+)	**3**	**5**	**2** (11+)	**1**
5	**2** (3+)	**1**	**4** (4)	**3**	**6**
4 (10+)	**3**	**6** (9+)	**1**	**5** (5)	**2** (13+)
3	**1** (5+)	**4**	**2**	**6**	**5**

65

6 (6)	**3** (7+)	**4**	**1** (8+)	**5**	**2**
2 (3+)	**1**	**5** (13+)	**6** (10+)	**4**	**3** (7+)
5 (8+)	**6** (11+)	**2**	**4** (6+)	**3**	**1**
3	**5**	**6**	**2**	**1** (3+)	**4** (10+)
1 (9+)	**4**	**3** (8+)	**5**	**2**	**6**
4	**2** (3+)	**1**	**3** (14+)	**6**	**5**

66

3 (5+)	**2**	**5** (6+)	**1**	**6** (14+)	**4**
1 (6+)	**5**	**3** (7+)	**6** (11+)	**4**	**2** (3+)
6 (9+)	**3**	**4**	**5**	**2** (7+)	**1**
2 (10+)	**4**	**1** (7+)	**3** (5+)	**5**	**6** (11+)
4	**1** (1)	**6**	**2**	**3** (7+)	**5**
5 (11+)	**6**	**2** (6+)	**4**	**1**	**3**

67

14+ 6	3	**5+** 4	1	**7+** 5	2
6+ 1	5	**4+** 3	**12+** 2	4	6
5	**3+** 2	1	**11+** 6	**3** 3	**7+** 4
9+ 4	1	**11+** 6	5	**9+** 2	3
2	**4** 4	5	**7+** 3	6	1
3	**8+** 6	2	4	**6+** 1	5

68

8+ 1	5	**15+** 6	2	4	3
2	**4** 4	**6+** 3	**15+** 1	5	6
11+ 6	**4+** 1	2	**18+** 5	3	**6+** 4
5	3	1	4	**7+** 6	2
9+ 3	2	4	6	1	**8+** 5
15+ 4	6	5	3	2	1

69

3+ 1	**11+** 5	**8+** 2	6	**10+** 4	3
2	6	**8+** 5	**6+** 1	3	**7+** 4
10+ 6	4	3	5	1	2
8+ 3	**3+** 2	1	**10+** 4	6	**11+** 5
5	**8+** 1	**13+** 4	3	**8+** 2	6
4	3	6	**2** 2	5	1

70

15+ 3	2	5	**7+** 1	6	**10+** 4
9+ 2	5	**10+** 4	6	**7+** 3	1
6	1	**3+** 2	**7+** 3	4	5
11+ 5	6	1	4	**3+** 2	**11+** 3
4 4	**11+** 3	**11+** 6	5	1	2
1	4	3	**7+** 2	5	6

71

13+ 5	**6+** 3	**5+** 4	1	**11+** 6	2
2	1	**8+** 5	**10+** 4	3	**15+** 6
6	2	3	5	1	4
9+ 3	6	**3+** 1	2	**10+** 4	5
15+ 4	5	6	3	2	1
5+ 1	4	**13+** 2	6	5	**3** 3

72

12+ 5	**3+** 2	1	**10+** 3	**12+** 4	6
1	**11+** 6	5	4	3	2
6	**8+** 5	3	**3+** 1	**8+** 2	**10+** 4
7+ 3	1	**6+** 4	2	6	5
10+ 4	3	2	**11+** 6	5	1
2	4	**11+** 6	5	**4+** 1	3

73

6 8+	**5** 8+	**2**	**4** 7+	**3**	**1** 1
2	**1**	**5** 15+	**6**	**4**	**3** 5+
5 15+	**6**	**4**	**3** 4+	**1**	**2**
4 7+	**3**	**6** 12+	**1**	**2** 8+	**5** 9+
1 6+	**2**	**3**	**5**	**6**	**4**
3 3	**4** 5+	**1**	**2** 13+	**5**	**6**

74

2 7+	**3** 3	**4** 9+	**5** 12+	**1**	**6**
4	**1**	**5**	**3** 9+	**6**	**2** 3+
6 11+	**4** 7+	**3**	**2** 8+	**5** 9+	**1**
5	**2** 3+	**1**	**6**	**4**	**3** 7+
3 9+	**5**	**6** 14+	**1** 3+	**2**	**4**
1	**6**	**2**	**4** 12+	**3**	**5**

75

3 14+	**6**	**5**	**2** 6+	**4**	**1** 6+
6 15+	**3** 3	**4** 10+	**5**	**1**	**2**
4	**2** 3+	**6** 7+	**1**	**5** 7+	**3**
5	**1**	**3** 7+	**4**	**2**	**6** 15+
1 6+	**5**	**2** 11+	**6**	**3**	**4**
2 10+	**4**	**1**	**3**	**6** 6	**5**

For Parents, Teachers, and Other Adults

KenKen puzzles were created by a Japanese educator, Tetsuya Miyamoto. In Japanese they are called KenKen, which translates as "cleverness squared." When I first learned about KenKen puzzles, I was intrigued. As a teacher of elementary and middle school mathematics for more than forty years, I became excited by their potential. And when I introduced them in several different grade levels, I was delighted to see how the puzzles instantly engaged students' interest and curiosity. Working on KenKen puzzles encourages children to concentrate and persevere.

Figuring out solutions to KenKen puzzles relies on basic math facts, thus providing beneficial practice in the context of solving puzzles. What I particularly like about these puzzles is that they also encourage children to think and reason mathematically, and to do so in their own ways. While each puzzle has one correct solution, there is no one "right" way to tackle it. In fact, I've found that I can solve the same problem in more than one way, depending on the order I use when choosing clues.

In some ways, KenKen puzzles are similar to the popular sudoku puzzles. Both involve filling in a grid with numbers, and both call for solutions without repeating numbers in the same row or column. But there is an important difference that makes KenKen puzzles particularly valuable for teaching mathematics. While numbers are used in sudoku puzzles, they are merely placeholder symbols; that is, the puzzles could use the letters of the alphabet, or pictures of fruit, or any other symbols, and the structure of the sudoku puzzles would still be the same. In KenKen puzzles, however, number relationships are integral to solutions. The puzzles in this book call for adding; puzzles in other I Can

KenKen! books call for adding *and* subtracting, or for multiplying. When solving KenKen puzzles, children get practice with basic arithmetic facts in a problem-solving context that provides a reason for using math.

The mechanics for the puzzles aren't complicated for children to learn. If you've not tried solving KenKen puzzles yourself, read through the introduction to familiarize yourself with the KenKen puzzles in this book. (I based this introduction on my actual experience introducing the puzzles in classrooms, and I've found that the introduction is also suitable for adults who are just getting started.)

An Additional Hint

Some puzzles include three-box shapes and clues that may initially stump children. For example, a 4×4 Addition KenKen puzzle might have a three-box L-shape with the Number Clue of 7, as in the upper left corner of this puzzle.

This clue means that the numbers in the three boxes have to add up to 7, using just the numbers 1, 2, 3, and 4, since these are the only numbers allowed in a 4×4 puzzle.

Encouraging children to come up with all of the possible combinations of addends is a useful strategy. Even for older children, for whom the addition is trivial, searching for all of the possibilities provides a chance to practice in a new way, calling for taking apart the quantity of 7 in different ways, and then deciding whether they've found all of the possible combinations. (For three numbers that add up to 7, without paying attention to the order of the numbers added, there are three different possible combinations: $1+2+4$, $2+2+3$, and $1+3+3$.)

It's also important for children to see that if any of the digits is repeated more than once, it cannot be placed in the corner of the L—otherwise the rule of not repeating same digit in a column or row is broken.

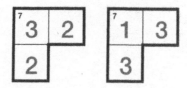

However, there are six possible ways to arrange the numbers when the addends are all different!

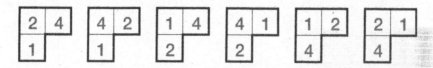

Notice also that in the same puzzle, there is another three-box shape with another Number Clue of 7—the rectangular shape in the right-side column. Here the only possibility is to use the numbers 1, 2, and 4, since you can't have a number repeat in the same column, and the challenge is to decide which number goes where. Try solving this KenKen puzzle.

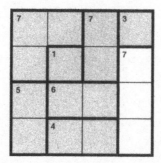

Investigating problems like these are not only good for children working on puzzles, but they also provide a platform for classroom math lessons that support mathematical thinking. Both in and out of the classroom, KenKen puzzles make a valuable contribution to students' learning. They help cement basic math facts, build number sense, promote logical thinking, build problem-solving skills, and motivate students mathematically in new and engaging ways.

Good luck with these KenKen puzzles!

—Marilyn Burns